BRITAIN

THE BOOK OF THE

MILLENNIUM

by Anthony Osmond-Evans

Foreword by Douglas Hurd

Published by The Beautiful Publishing Division
of Good Connections

FOREWORD

by Douglas Hurd

I was filming in New York recently with an American cameraman who had worked with the BBC for many years in the United States. Not long ago, he decided to visit Britain for the first time. His connection with the BBC led him to believe that he knew a good deal about the country and it was time he saw it for himself. I asked him for his main impression. He paused for a moment and said, surprisingly, "It's so big". It turned out that he had expected Britain to be about the size of the State of Connecticut.

As he talked about his visit, it became clear that what had really struck him most forcibly was the variety of Britain – the way in which you can travel thirty or forty miles and find yourself, even now at the end of the twentieth century, in a different landscape, with different architecture, listening to different voices.

Anthony Osmond-Evans, who has already produced two marvellous books on China and India, once again demonstrates his skills to the full as a photographer and compiler of beauty. He has found no less diversity within the geographical limits of his own country than he did in those two vast sub-continents. *Britain – The Book of the Millennium*, with pictures from some of Britain's most distinguished photographers will, I believe, act as an invaluable time-capsule. It will remind the generations who come after us of the wonders of the natural and man-made beauty of the United Kingdom at the end of the twentieth century and it will stand as a pictorial record of many of the physical achievements that we have accomplished by the end of this century, cautioning those who come after to guard the heritage of Britain that we will have passed on to them.

A perfect example of the surprising changes that can take place in our landscape occurs as you enter the Cotswolds from the east following the road from London through Oxford. Suddenly, you find yourself on a ridge running beside a gentle valley. Down on your right, the River Windrush meanders past a string of grey stone villages set close together. Each village has a sizeable church. There is one tiny church alone in a field with a Roman pavement below the chancel, which shows that the Romans too had an eye for a pleasant place to live. Finally, the spire of Burford Church comes into view, set in a pattern of hills and woods exactly suited to the landscape painter. Indeed, this is postcard country, what every foreign visitor believes England to be, and what as a matter of fact it often is. Certainly, I am biased having represented this part of England for more than twenty years in the House of Commons. Tastes vary, but for me, it is at its best in the soft light of a spring evening when the daffodils stand in contrast against the grey cottage walls.

Contrast the bustle of urban Newcastle, city of football, pubs and modern noise. Its university and main shopping centre, both near the heart of the city, belong to the twentieth century. The streets, which tumble down to the River Tyne, and the river front itself are a bewildering mixture of old and new. Newcastle, like the whole of the north-east of England, seemed in theory to lose its existence with the collapse of the coal and shipbuilding industries, which were its main livelihood. But new industry has come in, much of it from Japan and Korea and, although unemployment is still high, the variety of jobs available has greatly increased. Anyone visiting Newcastle today will be struck by its bustle and vitality.

In other parts of the United Kingdom, the contrasts can be even sharper. On boyhood holidays, I learned to relish the difference between the natural splendour of sea and mountains in the West Highlands and the rough man-made beauty of Edinburgh. Much later, working in Northern Ireland, I find myself within an hour of leaving industrial

Belfast walking through the sweeping emptiness of the Mountains of Mourne to the sea – one of the hidden treasures of our nation. This century has tried to put its harmonising hand on our country as well as the rest of the world. Petrol stations and fast food restaurants look much the same anywhere. But you do not have to move far from the main road in Britain to realise that this uniformity is more apparent than real, concealing the essential variety of the country but not destroying it.

It makes sense to probe a little deeper. Of course the Cotswold villages were not invented in order to make picture postcards. Those sturdy barns, substantial village houses and richly decorated churches are evidence of a woollen industry just as tough and successful in the Middle Ages as were the coal and shipbuilding industries which built Newcastle in the nineteenth century. Nor do my former constituents in the Cotswolds rely for their livelihood on selling antiques or serving tea and ice-cream to tourists. Behind the old facades of the blanket mills, for example a host of small industries are supplying technology and modern services to customers across the world

Whether in Scotland, Wales, Northern Ireland, Newcastle or the Cotswolds, Britain has to wrestle with the relationship between the old and the new. There have been times since the last War, when it looked as if we were going to make a mess of this. During the 60s and 70s, there were politicians who talked of 'ripping the heart out of our great cities'. Planners felt that they could only provide a worthwhile modern life for the people of Britain by sweeping away the slums and concentrating on high-rise flats and urban motorways. The wounds thus inflicted, not just on Britain's townscapes and countryside, but also on the health of our society, have not yet healed – but at least they are by and large no longer being inflicted. Luckily, my own market town of Witney did not have money to spend when the destructive fashion was at its height. By the time they had the resources, the mood had changed, so our modern shops find their place in a winding pedestrian street, where each building has a relationship with its neighbour and a scale suited for human beings. Look at what is happening in Newcastle today, or in Bristol or in Birmingham or Edinburgh. It is not easy to correct quickly the

mistakes of the recent past, but by and large they are not being repeated. Our planners are learning that it is possible for a city to change and meet new needs without abruptly cutting its links with the past.

The same is true of the countryside. London journalists regularly write as if the whole English countryside has been destroyed and a way of life

with it. Sitting in my garden, listening to the English songbirds, looking out over the unchanged countryside, I read in my newspaper that all these things have disappeared. I read likewise of the gradual decline of the Church of England as I return from a service in our tiny church. Yet it is twice as well attended as it would have been twenty years ago. Of course, in rural England too there has been radical change, some of it mistaken. The struggle for the right balance continues – but the arguments are now tilting the right way.

The search for the right balance between tradition and change goes wider than the physical environment. British political life is hard-hitting and politicians are in the habit of hailing their own efforts as a revolution compared to the inactivity of their backward looking opponents. Thus in recent years, we have had the 'Thatcher Revolution' and the 'Blair Revolution'. In fact, British institutions, like the British landscape, have been in a constant state of flux for centuries. The Victorian era, for example, which is sometimes treated by shallow commentators as an age of reaction, positively bubbled with change of all kinds. None of our political controversies in this century has matched the fury of the debates about the Reform Bill of

1832, the Repeal of the Corn Laws in 1846 or Home Rule for Ireland in 1886. Those arguments and the changes which they brought about make our own political volcanoes look small and spluttering by comparison. Politicians in Britain know that they have to pursue change within a certain framework, which includes the Monarchy, two Houses of Parliament and a recognition of the distinct character of the four parts of our Kingdom – England, Scotland, Wales and Northern Ireland. Within that framework, the balance will be constantly shifting, but the framework itself remains secure.

Everywhere in Britain you will find reminders of our links with the rest of the world. Britain has never been an isolationist country for the simple reason that neither our security nor our prosperity would be safe if we cut ourselves off from others. Here too, the balance has changed from time to time. In the seventeenth and eighteenth centuries, we were essentially a European power developing interests overseas but concentrating most of our effort on keeping a reasonable balance of power on the Continent of Europe. In the nineteenth and early twentieth centuries, we were an imperial power, exercising for a brief period an extraordinary sway over India, the rest of Asia, Africa and the Middle East. Now the Empire has been changed into a Commonwealth. Britain's role is presently as a partner rather than a ruler, but the Commonwealth partnership continues to affect the lives of millions

of our people. Our attention has shifted back to Europe. The European debate has taken the place of the Irish debate as the most complex in our national life. It is essentially a debate not about whether Britain is pro-Europe or anti-Europe, which is a meaningless question, but about the kind of Europe which suits Britain best. Partly because of this debate, one important change in recent years has gone unnoticed. When I first joined the Foreign Office as a young diplomat in 1952, and for many years thereafter, it was clear to everyone that the strength of Britain was in decline. We had exhausted ourselves in winning the War and in the economic mistakes of the immediate post-War government. Our Empire and our overseas investments were gradually running down.

The job of policy makers was to preside as successfully as possible over this decline, preventing it leading to the kind of breakdown which afflicted the French when tackling the problem of Algeria. At the end of the 70s this phase came to an end, marked by the settlement of the Rhodesia question, followed by the recovery of the Falkland Islands from the Argentine invasion.

Today, Britain is no longer in decline, either economically or politically. On the contrary, she has achieved a settled position as a successful medium-sized power, turning to increasingly good effect her fundamental assets, the skills of her people, her multicultural society and her sense of justice and fair play. Some of these assets are traditional and are being marketed worldwide, for example, the professionalism of our armed services in a world peace-keeping role. Our scientists in the domains of medicine and high technology have an outstanding reputation for innovation and the stature of our financial institutions in the realms of privatisation and deregulation is unsurpassed. There is now a reasonable consensus among the political parties in Britain on these issues, which should guarantee a continuity of our fundamental effort as a nation into the next century.

At the dawn of the new millennium, we in Britain can look back with pride at our achievements and look forward with a profound level of mature confidence to the future.

THE RT HON LORD HURD OF WESTWELL, CH CBE PC.

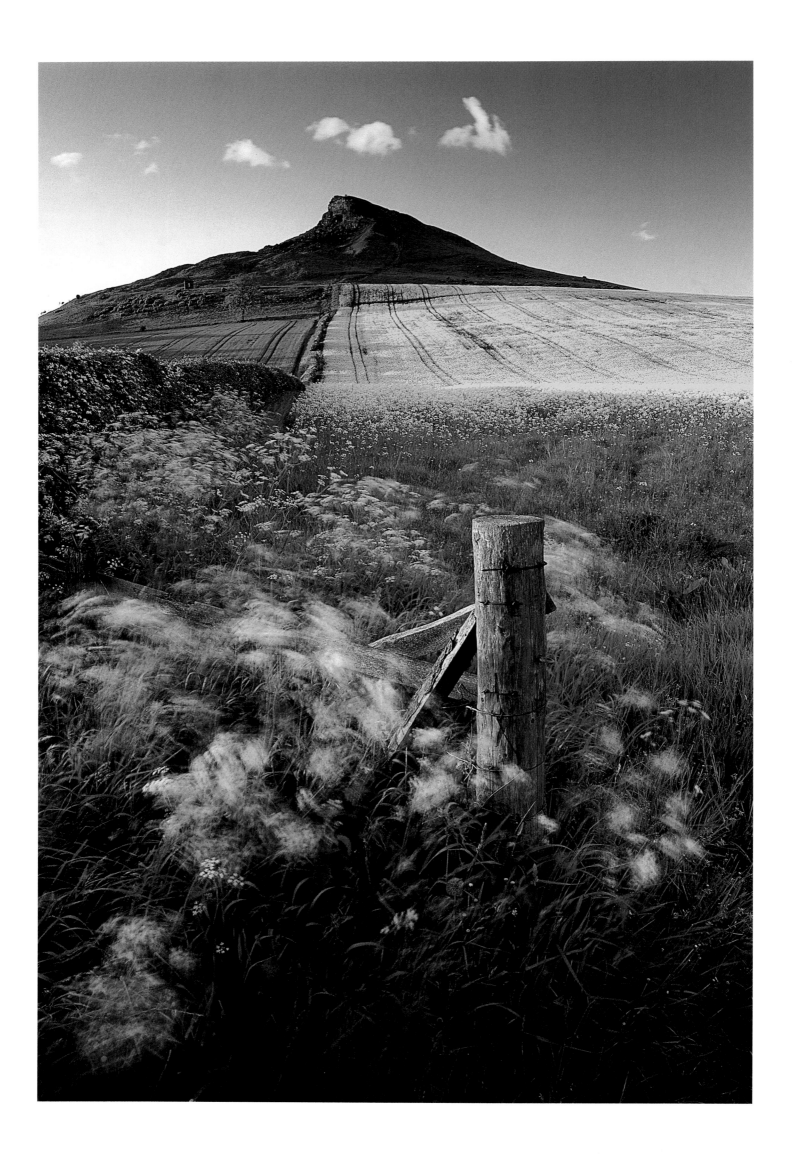

INTRODUCTION

The idea for *Britain – The Book of the Millennium* came to me in 1996 when photographing Mount Kachenjunga in the Himalayas, for my book *India the Beautiful*, which celebrated fifty years of India's independence. Having also photographed in China, South America and Europe, I thought it would be interesting to complete my trilogy of books with one on my own country at the millennium.

As a schoolboy at Tonbridge I used to sit at a desk on which the initials E.M.F. were engraved. Later, I learnt they had been carved by the great E.M. Forster, author of *A Passage to India*. Little did I dream that one day I, too, would produce books featuring India and Britain which would, I hope, give pleasure to others.

Britain – The Book of the Millennium is a photographic reflection of what I have found important, beautiful, or valuable during my own half century of life. The pictures follow the flow of the seasons; they resonate with the colours and textures of city and countryside, evoking the quintessential character – and eccentricity – of the British people. I share the honours of contributing to this book with some outstanding photographers and we trust our pictures will inspire, perhaps enthral, both for their beauty and for their fascinating subjects.

It is the third book that Lorraine has helped me create during this decade. I owe her my enduring gratitude for her sensitive, artistic judgment, her patience, and her practical good sense. She has been a precious partner in our

Lorraine Felkin

adventures around the world. I could not have achieved this book without her.

To my contemporaries and to me, Britain is Great, both for her political, industrial, scientific and cultural achievements and for her diversity of peoples, past and present. Douglas Hurd observes that Britain is a 'large country', for so much is packed into so small a space. There is an over-abundant choice for a picture editor. This book presents a selective view of the traditional heritage of Britain, from splendours to quaint customs, like Horn Dancing, Conker Championships, or the 800-year old daily Ceremony of the Keys at the Tower of London, uninterrupted even in war. Where else, but in the country that gave the world the English language, could you better such village names as Upper Snodgrass or Piddlehinton?

In stark contrast are the 'Space Age' designs of Canary Wharf and influential modern architects like Sir Norman Foster and Lord Richard Rogers, with his innovative Lloyds Building and Millennium Dome.

Our classical music heritage offers the peerless compositions of Purcell and Tallis, the rural reflections of Vaughan Williams, and the spiritual depths of today's John Tavener, recalling the purity of Gregorian plain chant. I feel especially at one with Elgar, imagining the haunting notes of his *Cello Concerto*, or *Nimrod*, from his *Enigma Variations*, echoing through Worcester Cathedral or soaring over the Malvern Hills. The opera at Glyndebourne, founded by John Christie and so successfully continued by his son, Sir George Christie, is a typically enjoyable British experience; who else but the British would dress up in a dinner jacket in daytime, to wait at Victoria Station (with a picnic hamper) for a train to the opera, in a country mansion in glorious grounds in Sussex – even in the rain?

As a nation, we embrace an extraordinary variety of sports, from Real (Royal) Tennis at historic venues

Edinburgh

Belfast

Cardiff

London

Jersey

0 10   50   100

Miles

33

45

69

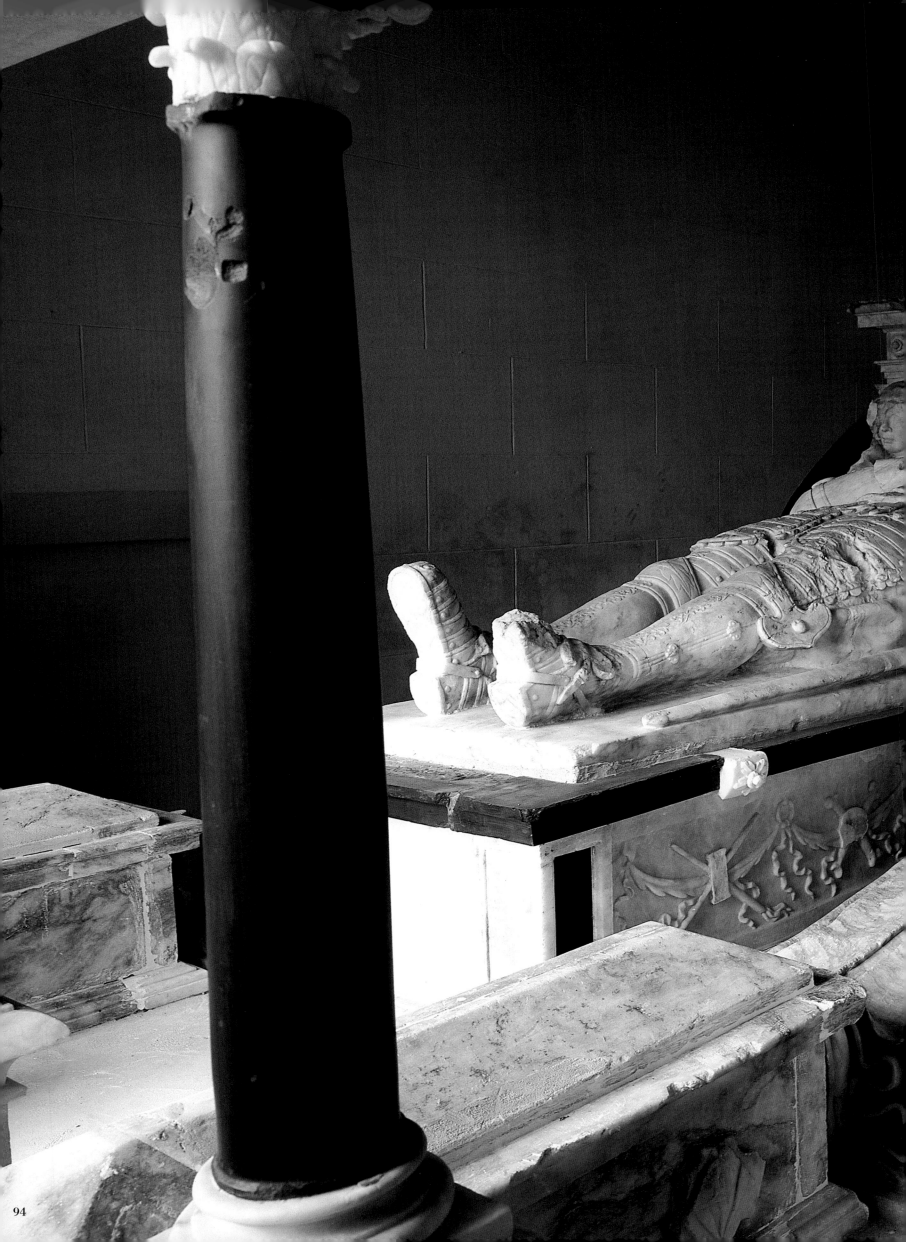

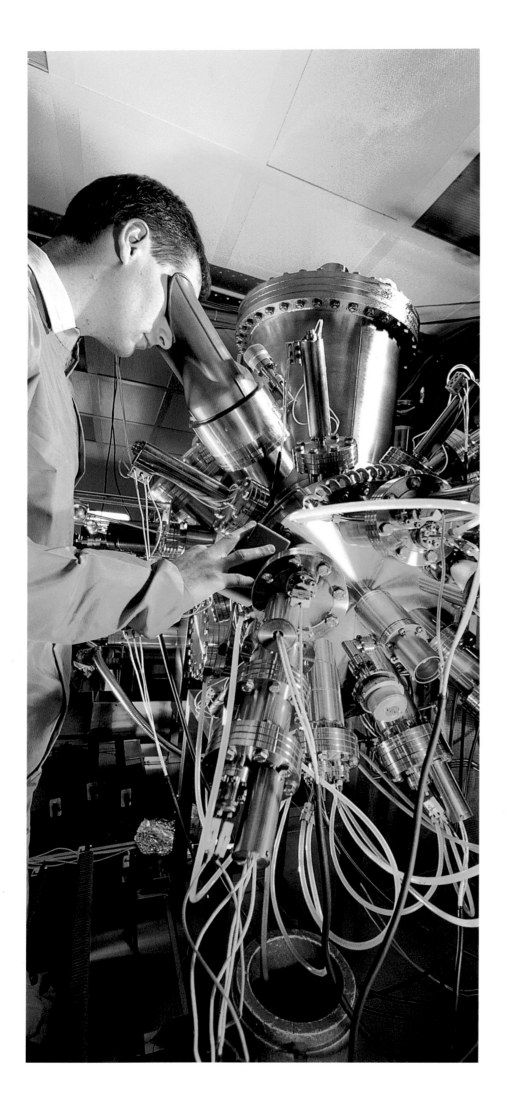

113

204
203

202

14th
LONDON SCOTTISH

LONDON
REGIMENT

167

THE PHOTOGRAPHS

2/3. Landewednack Church at dawn. The Lizard. *(Cornwall)*

4. Spring Daffodils at Southrop. Southrop Manor is in the background. The Cotswolds *(Gloucestershire)*

6/7. Shaftesbury. *(Dorset)*

8/9. The Lord Mayor's Show. John Chalstrey, newly Lord Mayor of London, waves to the crowd from his 18th century coach. The procession is escorted by Pikemen of the Honourable Artillery Company, the oldest regiment in Britain. The route is from his official residence, the Mansion House in the City, to the Law Courts in Westminster where he will pledge loyalty to the Sovereign. He has stopped en route at St Paul's Cathedral, to attend a service of dedication. *(London)*

10. Roseberry Topping rises 1051ft above the North Yorkshire Moors. *(North Yorkshire)*

11. Lorraine Felkin, Kilimani *(Jersey)*

12. The football caps of Benjamin Howard-Baker. Amateur footballer and athlete, he was the Corinthian Football Club's goal keeper 1921-1923. A member of Britain's Athletics team at the Stockholm Olympics (1912) and Antwerp (1922). Holder of the British high jump record of 6' 5", (1921 to 1947). *(Powys)*

13. Jellybean jar with scoop. This unusual piece of ceramic art, by potter Morgan Hall, appears to have been influenced by Sir John Tenniel's illustration of the caterpillar's 'hookah' in Lewis Carroll's *Alice in Wonderland.* *(Cardiff)*

13. Horace or Henrietta (a prickly job to establish) takes supper in our garden in Jersey. I have since learned that tinned cat food and water are best for hedgehogs.

14. Statue of Sir Francis Drake on Plymouth Hoe. The first Englishman to sail around the world, he later defeated the Spanish Armada in 1588. He was knighted by Queen Elizabeth I on the deck of his ship, *The Golden Hind.* *(Devonshire)*

15. Map of the United Kingdom & Northern Ireland, in pewter.

16. Bluebells at the Winkworth Arboretum near Munstead Wood, Godalming. *(Surrey)*

17. Punting on the Backs of the River Cam at Cambridge, Britain's second oldest university. *(Cambridgeshire)*

18/19. Daffodils at Hever Castle. Restored with its maze this century by Lord Astor and now open to the public. In the 16th century it was one of the childhood homes of Queen Anne Boleyn, the executed second wife of Henry VIII and mother of Queen Elizabeth I. *(Kent)*

20/21. John Birth fly fishing for trout on the River Test. *(Hampshire)*

22. 'Horseguards' from across the lake in St James's Park. The lake was created for Charles II in the 17th century. Many of the ducks (and Pelicans) can trace their ancestry from that time. *(London)*

23. The Laburnum Grove at Bodnant, home of Lord Aberconway, former President of the Royal Horticultural Society. The gardens have been donated to the National Trust. *(Conwy)*

24/25. Fields of rape near St Germans. *(Cornwall)*

26/27. Old boats drawn up on the edge of the River Avon's oyster beds near Bigbury Bay. *(Devonshire)*

28. Askrigg. This small 18th century village in Wensleydale was used for the popular TV series *All Creatures Great and Small* by the late Alf Wight, the vet who wrote under the pen-name James Herriot. *(North Yorkshire)*

29. The centuries-old craft of dry stone walling creates a green mosaic in Weardale. *(North Yorkshire)*

30. A young girl, bewitching and bewitched, in the enchanted Newton Wood. *(North Yorkshire)*

31. The Fairy Glen situated near Betws-y-coed, North Wales. *(Conwy)*

32. Emma Woodhead wears an Andie MacDowell style hat from British hit film, *Four Weddings and a Funeral,* co-starring Hugh Grant. She is a guest at the wedding of Holly Kelvin-Davies and Charles Wordie in St Albans. *(Hertfordshire)*

33. Mrs Michaela Wright, sister of the groom, breastfeeding three week-old Fenella at the reception of the same wedding. *(Hertfordshire)*

34. A future bardic harpist perhaps? This little boy was caught by the camera at 1998's Eisteddfod at Bridgend. *(Glamorganshire)*

35. Dame Kiri Te Kanawa sings whilst at the harp during Richard Strauss's *Capriccio* at Glyndebourne. *(East Sussex)*

36/37. May Morning celebration on Magdalen College tower, Oxford. Choristers sing madrigals and hymns at 6.00 am. Students gather below on Magdalen Bridge after partying all night.

38. A young girl in Northern Ireland demonstrates her ability at traditional Irish Dancing.

39. 'With mallet aforethought?' Mr Rolfe of Budleigh Salterton is about to hit his ball through a hoop during a keenly-fought croquet match against arch-rivals, Sidmouth. *(Devonshire)*

40. Studying the Form, despite the Garrick Club hat-band, this elderly couple at 'Glorious Goodwood' clearly need a little help from *The Sporting Life.* *(West Sussex)*

41. The Derby, named after the 12th Earl of Derby, is Britain's premier flat race. It has been run over one and a half miles at Epsom every June since 1780. One racegoer looks as if he has 'lost his shirt', while the other gentleman is in danger of losing his trousers. *(Surrey)*

42. Yvonne Evans is a familiar sight in Fishguard. Seen here re-enacting the part of heroic Welsh heroine Jemima Nicholls. In 1797 she led a group of local women which put a French invasion force to flight. The redoubtable Jemima herself rounded up 12 prisoners with her pitchfork. Her costume was designed by David Emmanuel, who with his wife, Elizabeth, created Princess Diana's wedding dress. *(Pembrokeshire)*

43. 18th century costume gives an authentic air at Stokesay castle near Ludlow on the English Welsh borders. *(Shropshire)*

44. The choir of Tonbridge School in the outer courtyard of the Hall of the Worshipful Company of Skinners, before the annual procession on Corpus Christi Day. The Skinners have been benefactors of Tonbridge since the school was founded by Sir Andrew Judd in 1553. The school's motto is *Deus dat incrementum* (God gives increase). *(London)*

45. Mr Hall, the Beadle of the Worshipful Company of Skinners, takes part in the annual Corpus Christi Day procession in London.

46. HM The Queen reviews the Household Brigade on her official Birthday Parade in June. Behind her, ride (L-R) The Prince of Wales, The Duke of Edinburgh, and The Duke of Kent – Colonels respectively of the Welsh, Grenadier and Scots Guards. *(London)*

47. Trooping the Colour. The Commanding Officer of the Irish Guards heads the parade on horseback. Behind him the Scots Guards, formed in 1642, are identified by the buttons set in threes on their scarlet tunics. All the foot soldiers of the Brigade of Guards, of which her Majesty is Colonel-in-Chief, wear these dress tunics and bearskin hats for ceremonial occasions. *(London)*

48. Chelsea Pensioners at the Queen's Birthday Parade. Charles II established Chelsea Hospital in 1682 to care for invalid pensioners of his recently formed Regular Army. Their bright full dress scarlet cloaks and black hats were designed in the early 18th century. Today the Chelsea Flower Show is held in the Hospital grounds and is the start of the English Social Season. *(London)*

49. The Ceremony of the Keys. Roderick Truelove, Yeoman Warder, accompanied by a military escort locks the gates of the Tower of London. This ancient ceremony has been carried out for 800 years, uninterrupted, through war and peace. Once the Tower is secured for the night, admission is by password only. *(London)*

50. The Hon. Mr Justice Tucker, in Lincoln's Inn. Senior Judge of the Queen's Bench Division of the High Court of Justice, Sir Richard Tucker was called to the bar by Lincoln's Inn in 1954, took Silk and became a QC in 1972. A Bencher of the Inn in 1979, he was appointed a Judge in 1985. *(London)*

51. The Town Crier of Lambeth leads a procession of 'professors' around the streets of Covent Garden at the Punch & Judy Festival in May. *(London)*

52/53. The Fourth of June at Eton College's annual private celebration of George III's birthday. Now a parents' day, with cricket matches, and exhibitions. Boater and flower-decked 'wet bobs' ship their oars and perilously stand, during 'The Procession of Boats' in which a dozen crews of all ages take part. At the command, "Hats off to Eton. Hats off to Windsor" crews salute both banks of the river Thames. Eton, founded in 1440, and currently attended by Princes William and Harry, arguably Britain's oldest, largest and most distinguished public school. *(Berkshire)*

54/55. Strawberries and cream at the Private Preview at the Royal Academy of Arts' annual Summer Exhibition at Old Burlington House, Piccadilly. The late Sir Roger Grey, past President, is in the centre wearing his insignia of office. From May to August 12th every year the Academy exhibits some 1,500 works from artists selected out of about 12,000. *(London)*

56. Her Majesty The Queen says farewell to the late Dean of St Paul's, The Very Reverend Eric Evans, following a service of Commemoration and dedication for the most distinguished Order of St Michael and St George. HRH The Duke of Kent, Grand Master of the Order, is at the rear. *(London)*

57. Her Majesty Queen Elizabeth The Queen Mother with Choristers from St Paul's Cathedral, after the Friends Festival. She has been patron of the Friends of St Paul's since 1952 and has attended every Festival for nearly 50 years. *(London)*

58. These 'three wise men' in bowler hats are judging foxhounds at the South of England Agricultural Show at Ardingly, which is held annually during the second week of June. *(West Sussex)*

59. Crufts Dog Show at Earls Court. Promotional girl, Katerina, from Stafford, has not quite succeeded in convincing these two splendid Dalmatians that she is one of them. Charles Cruft 1852-1938, a British dog expert, organised his first dog show in 1886 in London, held annually ever since. *(London)*

60. Matriculation Day, Magdalen College. New undergraduates are photographed before processing to the Sheldonian Theatre. The boys wear white ties and dark suits with their gowns; the girls wear black ties. Their expressions suggest it has been a busy Freshers' week. *(Oxfordshire)*

61. PC at No 10 Downing Street, the home of the Prime Minister. *(London)*

62/63. Henley Royal Regatta Two 'eights' duel it out at the 1⅛ mile post on the River Thames. On the far side can be seen Phyllis Court which is famed for its hospitality. *(Berkshire)*

64. The engine driver has an early morning cup of tea as his engine builds up a head of steam on the Ffestiniog railway. Still in use as a tourist attraction, this little mountain railway was built in the 19th century to carry slate from the quarries at Blaenau Ffestiniog. *(Gwynedd)*

65. Coal fired steam traction engines began to replace cart horses at the end of the 19th century, prior to the introduction of modern tractors. Today, they can be seen at well-attended steam rallies all over Britain. Brassington. *(Peak District)*

66/67. Blacksmith, Bernard Tidmarsh, shoes a customer's horse. His family have also been wheelwrights at the Crudwell forge in Wiltshire for 400 years. Since 1952, Mr Tidmarsh has attended horses of the Royal Family and Olympic riders. It was through Prince Charles that Mr Tidmarsh met his wife, one of the Prince's grooms. *(Wiltshire)*

68/69. The Sexton's King Charles spaniel looks up adoringly at him. He waits to toll the bells behind a spider's web of ropes at St Mary's Church, Eardisland. *(Herefordshire)*

70. John Sangster, aka 'Biggles' in his 'Blower', a beautifully maintained 1928 supercharged Bentley, at a Bentley owners' meet, Wentworth Golf Club. *(Berkshire)*

71. HRH The Prince of Wales is warmly greeted on the morning of his 50th birthday during a walkabout in Sheffield. *(South Yorkshire)*

72/73. Sammy and Sue. Two locals have a drink with a friend at the Balmoral public house in Preston. *(Lancashire)*

74. The Royal Crescent, Bath was built in the 18th century by John Wood. At this time Bath developed into a fashionable spa. In 1781, the astronomer William Herschel discovered the planet Uranus, famous visitors include the novelist Jane Austen. *(Avon)*

75. Stilton cheeses mature in the Hartington Creamery store. Stilton is still largely produced in the Melton Mowbray area, but its name comes from a village just to the south of Peterborough where, in coaching days, it was taken en route to London. *(Derbyshire)*

76. Senior citizens take a nap in the late Summer sun on the Promenade along the sea front at Eastbourne. *(Sussex)*

77. Conker Championship at the village of Long Ashton. The traditional schoolboy game is fought by the World Champion with deadly seriousness against competitors bedecked in unique conker (horse chestnut) garlands. *(Northamptonshire)*

78/79. Wiltons Restaurant, Jermyn Street. One of London's legendary restaurants, world famous for its seafood, especially oysters. Dining are former Rackets champions C.T.M. (Tom) Pugh, past Captain of Gloucestershire Cricket Club and Charles Swallow with his wife Susanna who run the Vanderbilt Club, favourite tennis venue of the late Princess Diana. Pat, the barman, probably knows as many secrets as anybody in London.

80. These London children are captivated by a performance at the annual Punch and Judy festival in which 'professors' gather to celebrate their skills and hold a service in St Paul's Church, Covent Garden. *(London)*

81. Mr Punch, the hump-backed, hook-nosed hand puppet is notorious for beating his wife, Judy, and outwitting all his opponents. *(London)*

82/83. Buckingham Palace Garden Party. HM The Queen usually arrives at 4.00 pm to the sound of the National Anthem. Here (bottom left) wearing green, she meets selected guests from the 8,000 invited annually. *(London)*

84/85. Londoners' cheerful day out at the Epsom Derby. Pearly Kings and Queens lead the singing of 'Rule Britannia' at Tattenham Corner. *(Surrey)*

86/87. Dray horses still deliver beer locally for Young & Co's Wandsworth Brewery. Their harness is being given a final adjustment before the start of the Easter Parade at Battersea Park. *(London)*

88/89. 'The Knighthood of the Old Green'. Southampton Bowling Club, the home of bowls, was established in 1299, giving this club the reputation of being the oldest bowling club in the world. *(Hampshire)*

90/91. Celebrating the Summer Solstice at Stonehenge. Ancient Druids believed in the immortality of the soul and reincarnation. They taught astronomy and engaged in human sacrifice. Their central religious rite involved the sacred oak tree from which they cut mistletoe with a golden knife. Modern Druidism is purely a 20th century re-creation. More than 4000 years old, Stonehenge is a world heritage site. *(Wiltshire)*

92. Cygnets ride on their mother's back as she floats serenely along the Union canal. *(Shropshire)*

attempted rape. Her uncle, St Beno restored her to life by replacing her head back on her body. The scar is visible on her neck. Holywell has the longest unbroken record of pilgrimages. Every year, from Whitsun to October, Catholics come from around the world to take water at the well and to pray for healing. *(Flintshire)*

99. The Interior of the Italian Chapel near the Churchill Barrier on Lamb Holm Island. This ornate chapel was built by Italian prisoners of war during World War II, inside a corrugated iron Nissen hut. Some of the ex POWs return every few years to carry out repairs and visit friends made during the war. *(Orkney)*

100. Death masks of 19th century hanged criminals on display in the Dungeons of Norwich Castle. In some cases it is possible to see the rope marks round their necks. The masks were taken as part of a contemporary research into phrenology. The degree of mental development was supposed to be indicated by the shape of the skull, reflecting the development of the underlying parts of the brain. *(Norfolk)*

Lorraine's dressing table with fresh Sweet Peas from the garden in Jersey.

93. Art class at the City and Guilds of London Art School Fine Art Painting Department. The juxtaposition of the live nude model and the skeleton make for an arresting composition. *(London)*

94/95. The alabaster tomb of William Bassett (1552-1601) in the Norman St Bartholomew's Church, Blore. Her Majesty Queen Elizabeth II is a direct descendant through eleven generations. Blore, population twelve, claims to be at the centre of England. *(Derbyshire)*

96. The dome of St Paul's Cathedral, from Cheapside. Sir Christopher Wren's masterpiece was rebuilt in 1717, following the Great Fire of London of 1666. *(London)*

97. Lincoln College Library, Oxford The College was founded in 1427, but the Library was only moved into the deconsecrated church of All Saints in the 1970s. *(Oxford)*

98. St. Winefride's Shrine, Holywell. A sixth century saint, her head was sliced off by Prince Caradoc after an

101. Albert Hodge who took up the position of butler, in 1933 when he was only 20, to the late General Lord Ismay, seen in the portrait. *(Berkshire)*

102/103. Ray Corne has been making riding hats since the age of 12, Pateys (London) Ltd produce made-to-measure riding hats, top hats and bowlers. He uses a conformateur, a spiked metal contraption designed in the last century, to copy the exact shape of his customers' heads. *(London)*

104/105. Farmers' Christmas Market at Knighton. At the final auction market before Christmas, local farmers fortify their tea with whisky. *(Powys)*

106. The Buchanan tartan kilt is worn here by Seoras (George) Wallace, the head of the Scottish Battle Clan Society. The traditional male costume of the Scottish Highlands since the 17th century consists of a kilt and, plaid, (a cloak worn over one shoulder). Accessories include a sporran (goatskin pouch), dirk or long dagger, cap, kilt pin and skiandubh

(pronounced 'skiandoo') a short dagger usually worn in the right stocking. *(Argyll and Bute)*

107. Laurence Blair Oliphant lives at Ardblair Castle on the outskirts of Blairgowrie and is Chieftain of the Blairgowrie Highland Games. The owner of the Ardblair Estates, he farms sheep and breeds Highland Cattle. *(Perthshire)*

108/109. A local band plays in a Northern Irish pub, providing a musical pointer to better and more peaceful times ahead.

110. The Semiconductor and Micro-Electronics Centre, (one of the Centres of Expertise) at the University of Wales, Cardiff. Wales, not least through the efforts of of the Welsh Development Agency, has taken advantage of the opportunities offered by the new technology industries. It has the highest concentration of Japanese-owned plants in the UK. *(Cardiff)*

111. The old Reading Room of the British Library built in 1857, as a part of the British Museum. Photographed on October 1997, the day it closed to the public for the last time before the move to new premises in Euston Road. It receives a copy of every book published in Britain, including this one, and contains over 10 million volumes. *(London)*

112. The new Lloyds Building, designed by architect Richard Rogers has won many awards for bold innovation. It houses one of Britain's most important financial institutions, named after the 17th century coffee house owned by Edward Lloyd, where insurance underwriters used to meet. Lloyds' business in marine, aviation and general insurance is worldwide and an important source of invisible earnings for Britain. *(London)*

113. Lincoln Cathedral from the ramparts. Construction began in 1075 and continued until the 15th century. It has the earliest Gothic work in Britain. *(Lincolnshire)*

114/115. Canary Wharf, in the last century, was an important part of the Port of London. The initial phase of the new development on the Isle of Dogs began in 1988. The first tenants arrived in 1991. When finally completed, early in the new millennium, Canary Wharf will be capable of accommodating up to 100,000 office workers. The tower is 800ft tall and the second highest in Europe. *(London)*

116/117. Westminster Abbey. All the English monarchs (except Edward V and Edward VIII) since William the Conqueror have been crowned here. On the left is Big Ben, a prominent part of The Houses of Parliament. *(London)*

118/119. Clifton Suspension Bridge over the river Avon at Bristol was built last century by Isambard Kingdom Brunel (1806-1859). *(Avon)*

120/121. Liverpool's two cathedrals are linked by Hope Street. The Anglican cathedral, Britain's largest ecclesiastical building, was built to a traditional gothic design by Sir Giles Gilbert Scott and only recently completed. The Roman Catholic Cathedral was finished in 1967 to the modern, in the round, design of Sir Frederick Gibberd. *(Merseyside)*

122/123. Storm clouds surround Castle Stalker, which overlooks the Sound of Shuna

Shakespeare at the Regent's Park Open Air Theatre in London.

towards Loch Linnhe, Port Appin on the west coast of Scotland. The family home of the Stewart Allwoods. *(Argyll and Bute)*

124/125. The ruined castle. Dunsborough, on the Northumberland coast, was once the mediaeval stronghold of the Dukes of Lancaster. It stands on the same basalt ridge of rock as Hadrian's Wall to the west. *(Northumberland)*

126/127. Kilchurn Castle, Loch Awe. This delightful, narrow west highland loch is 23 miles long. The ruined castle, originally built in 1440, lies not far from the northern shore near the main Glasgow to Oban road. To the left is Glen Strae. *(Argyll and Bute)*

128/129. A misty morning presents a splendid panorama towards England from Bristly Ridge in Snowdonia. *(Gwynedd)*

130. Charles and Fiona Calvert steal a kiss as they cut the cake during their wedding reception at Hazlewood Castle. *(North Yorkshire)*

131. Aston Martin DB7. The Best of British comes to rest by Lake Buttermere in the Lake District. *(Cumbria)*

132. Denzil Davies demonstrates the ancient skill of handling a coracle on the Afon Teifi at Cenarth. These traditional round fishing boats, probably of Celtic origin, are made of wickerwork or laths over which a waterproofed animal skin is stretched and fitted. *(Carmarthenshire)*

133. A peaceful afternoon sketching at Llyswen near the river Wye. *(Powys)*

134/135. The Manor House, Lower Brockhampton stands on an island surrounded by a moat. It was built at the end of the 14th century. Much of it, including the Great Hall, has remained unchanged. *(Herefordshire)*

136/137. The estuary at Salcombe provides a safe anchorage for hundreds of yachts and small boats. *(Devonshire)*

138/139. The Appleby Horse Fair is held every year in the ancient market town. Horses and foals splash through the waters of the river Eden. *(Cumbria)*

140. The green of the short 17th, on the Edinburgh (South) course at Wentworth Golf Club. *(Berkshire)*

141. A Harrods horse-drawn delivery van stops in London's Belgrave Square. *(London)*

142. Winner of the Silver Arrow, Charles Horsefall, a verdurer of the Woodmen of Arden, feted by his fellow archers after the morning's Grand Ward Mote, at the forest ground of Meriden. *(Warwickshire)*

143. Morris Dancers at St Edmonds of Abingdon The Mayor of Ock Street holds the silver sword and the wooden loving cup decorated with silver hearts. Elected for the day, he wears the sash of office whilst his companions dance around him in celebration. *(Oxfordshire)*

144. The peaceful little Strangford ferry port opposite Portaferry, at the entrance of Strangford Lough. The ferry connects the road from Downpatrick to Newtonards and Belfast along the eastern lakeside route. *(County Down)*

145. Neil Bruce Copp holding a lobster pot at Ilfracombe harbour. Originally a fishing and farming family, the Bruce Copps subsequently provided transport for passengers and cargo along the North Devon coast by means of horse-drawn carriages, and later motorised charabancs. Museum records show the family to have been the foremost developers of the town, one of whom, Thomas Bruce Copp, was mayor in 1882. *(Devonshire)*

146/147. Earl Grey's Elegy? Spectators at Henley Royal Regatta take time out for tea in the churchyard of St Mary the Virgin, Henley-on-Thames. *(Oxfordshire)*

148/149. "Village cricket in the summertime is a delight to everyone", Lord Denning. The cricket pitch at Tilford with the Barley Mow pub. *(Surrey)*

150/151. The Falls of Dochart. The river Dochart runs into Loch Tay at Killin. The Dochart Bridge, built in 1760 was repaired in 1830 and is on the main road for travellers heading along the picturesque banks of Loch Tay. *(Stirling)*

152/153. Chevening House, near Sevenoaks, is the official country residence of the Foreign Secretary. It was completed in 1630 to the design of Inigo Jones and purchased in 1717 by the 1st Earl Stanhope. In 1967 the house, with 3,000 acres, was left to the nation by the 7th Earl. The Prince of Wales lived there from 1974-1980. It has since been occupied by every Foreign Secretary from Lord Barber to the present incumbent, Robin Cook. *(Kent)*

154. Cardiff winning a rugby match against arch rivals Llanelli. *(Cardiff)*

155. Arsenal defends against Newcastle United and England's captain Alan Shearer, at Arsenal's Highbury ground. Arsenal went on to win the match, the FA Cup and the League in 1998. *(London)*

156/157. Richard Williams MFH with Geoff Hughes huntsman above Bedel Gelert, Snowdonia. *(Gwynedd)*

158/159. The Glenfinnen Viaduct (Invernesshire)

160. The Cumbrian mountain express has just left Garsdale. *(North Yorkshire)*

161. Wast Water to the Screes, Leaconfield Commons. *(Cumbria)*

162/163. A member of the Beaufort Hunt waits at a covert. *(Gloucestershire)*

164/165. Rockingham Castle, Market Harborough, was built by William the Conqueror and used by the kings of England until 1530. It is still the Saunders Watson family home. Charles Dickens is said to have seen the ghost of Lady Dedlock pass through the 400 year-old yew hedge. The Roundheads stormed the castle in 1643. *(Leicestershire)*

166/167. 'Lest we forget'. Thousands of wooden crosses planted in the grounds of Westminster Abbey commemorate the dead of two world wars and other 20th century conflicts. Taken on the eve of Remembrance Day, which is the Sunday nearest every November 11th. *(London)*

168. Fireworks at Lewes. An elaborate replica of Guy Fawkes explodes and burns on one of the November 5th bonfires commemorating the Gunpowder Plot, which in 1605, set out to blow up the Houses of Parliament. *(East Sussex)*

169 More fireworks. Someone is having fun at Cirencester Agricultural College's end of year ball. *(Gloucestershire)*

170. Real Tennis at Lords; David Cull, the head professional in play. This complex game originated in France in the 12th century. The heavy balls are made of layered cloth around a core. Many of these cores were cut from material of the original tunics worn last century during the Crimean War. As in ordinary tennis the ball is hit from end to end, but in Real Tennis the sloping roof (penthouse) and side walls can be used. Prince Edward and some 2000 people in the UK play at 24 courts, including Hampton Court Palace and the grand private houses of Petworth and Hatfield. *(London)*

171. The 7.42 from Moreton-in-Marsh to Paddington travelling at speed over the level crossing at Bruern Abbey, near Churchill. In Victorian times the train was obliged to stop to unload passengers and collect the mail bag. *(Oxfordshire)*

172/173. Eric Edwards has been Marshman to the Broads Authority's How Hill Nature Reserve at Ludham since 1967 and has responsibility for harvesting the Norfolk reed and sedge as a local source of supply for traditional thatching. *(Norfolk)*

174/175. Blen Cathra mountain and the Threlkeld Valley. *(Cumbria)*

176/177. Beech trees at Dunkeld. Sunlight filters through the mist on a frosty October morning. *(Perthshire)*

178/179. Heather bedecks the foothills of these wonderful mountains Canisp and Suilven. Among the oldest in the world, they are composed of Torridon Sandstone and lie behind Lochinver, a fishing village on the west coast of Scotland. *(Highland)*

180/181. The Commando Memorial at Skearn Bridge, Fort William. *(Highland)*

182/183. The Thames Barrier protects London from flooding during periods of tidal surges in the North Sea. When a flood threat is imminent, the gates take 30 minutes to swing up to a vertical position and form a continuous barrier. High-Point Rendel Ltd was responsible for extensive hydrological and tidal investigations, hydraulic and model studies, engineering design, supervision of construction and initial commissioning.

184/185. The Library at Chatsworth. In 1815, the 6th Duke of Devonshire converted the Long Gallery to a library. The bookcases were designed by his architect, Sir Jeffry Wyatville (1830). There are altogether over 17,000 books here and in the adjoining ante-library. The painting on the easel is Henry VIII after Holbein. *(Derbyshire)*

186/187. The Dining Room at Weston Park (the home of the Earls of Bradford), was formed about 100 years ago from several small rooms. In 1968, redecoration was undertaken under the direction of the present Earl's mother. The finest pictures hang here including many portraits by Van Dyck. *(Shropshire)*

188/189. Harlech Castle, now an historic ruin overlooking Cardigan Bay, was built in 1285 by Edward I. *(Gwynedd)*

190/191. A skier takes off during one of the runs under Ben Nevis, Britain's highest mountain at 4,406ft. *(Highland)*

192/193. A pheasant shoot on a private estate. *(Lancashire)*

194/195. Red Deer & Highland Stag in the snow 1,000 feet up in the Ardverikie Forest above Loch Laggan. Before the sun rose it was -20° C. *(Invernesshire)*

196. Snowdon, unusually snow covered, is Wales' highest mountain at 3,560 ft. A rack and pinion railway takes travellers from Llanberis to its peak, Y Wyddfa. The surrounding area, Snowdonia, was designated a National Park in 1951. *(Gwynedd)*

199. Llywelyn ap Iorwerth's statue in Conwy. The Prince of Gwynedd supported the English barons against his father-in-law, King John of England, obtaining recognition for Welsh rights in Magna Carta during the year 1215. *(Conwy)*

THE PHOTOGRAPHERS

A.O-E. 2/3, 4, 11, 12, 13, 15, 16, 22, 23, 32, 33, 39, 42, 43, 44, 45, 46, 47, 48, 49, 50, 54/55, 61, 70, 78/79, 92, 94/95, 97, 116/117, 122/123, 130, 131, 132, 133, 134/135, 140, 141, 142, 144, 145, 152/153, 154, 155, 170, 171, 180/181, 198 &199.
Stephen Brayne. 13.
Canary Wharf plc. 114/115.
Joe Cornish. 10, 28, 29, 30, 124/125 & 174/175.
Paul Chapells/Sheffield Star. 71.
Richard Davies. 35.
Simon Everett. 14, 65, & 156/157.
Lorraine Felkin. 24/25 & 136/137.
John Hamilton. 15.
Rowan Isaac. 6/7 & 200.
Jill Jennings/Christopher Hill Photographic Library. 38 & 108/109.
Peter Karry. 51, 80, 81 & 86/87.
John McPherson. 158/159.
Alex McNeil/Stewart McColl. 112.
Nick Meers/courtesy of the British Museum 110.
Dave Newbould. 31, 64, 128/129, 188/189 & 196.
D. Sellman. 18/19.
John Slater. 100, 113, 118/119, 120/121, 166/167 & 184/185.
Michael Powell/Times Newspapers. 77.
Skyscan. 164/165.
Homer Sykes/Network Photographers. 36/37, 40, 41, 52/53, 58, 59, 60, 62/63, 72/73, 76, 82/83, 84/85, 88/89, 90/91, 98, 99, 104/105, 106, 138/139, 143, 146/147, 148/149, 162/163, 168/169, 182/183, 192/193 & 200.
Nigel Tyrrell. 96.
Simon Upton/Country Life Picture Library. 66/67, 68/69, 101, 102/103 & 172/173.
Simon Upton/The World of Interiors. 93.
Dan Wales. 75.
Philip Way. 8/9, 56 & 57.
Advances Wales. 111.
Ronnie Weir. 107, 126/127, 150/151, 176/177, 178/179, 190/191 & 194/195.
Weston Park. 186/187.
David Williams. 34, 74 & 199.
Jim Winkley. 160.

ACKNOWLEDGMENTS

Director of Design: Mike Norriss
Design team at A4: Gary Bigwood, Kim Spickett, John Higginbottom and Lisa Vincent.
The Design team in Jersey: Major Alan and Betty Barnes, Maurice Wheller, Carol Wood and our hedgehog.

The Fens

Editorial: George Metcalfe.
Advice: Julie Ronald.
Audrey Stevenson.
Proof-reader: Jon Sargent
Origination & technical: *Britain – The Book of the Millennium* was produced using QuarkXPress, Adobe Illustrator & Photoshop, Xerox Splash colour proofs.
Separations: Alan Wright and his production team headed by Bill Robson & Colin Howell at Magnet Harlequin.
Printed: By Arnoldo Mondadori Editore on Komori Lithrone 50 press, size 97 × 130cm.
Paper: Larius Brillante 150g/m2 from Cartiere Burgo.
Inks by: BASF Vernici e Inchiostri SpA.
  Administrative Assistance: Sue Jobson. Jean Jones, Don McGregor and Derek Hawkins of Good Connections. Sue Garfield and Sharon Feldman-Vazan, of The Organisers. Carole Ashford.
  Photographic Assistance: Kodak; Nick Fox and Dr Christopher Toombs.
  Optikos: Tony Speight and Colin Toovey.

Photographic Equipment: Mamiya provided by David Vaughan & Mike Edwards of Johnson's Photopia
Finance: To the Bank Manager, a suitable thank-you.
Portrait of Anthony Osmond-Evans by courtesy of the late Sir David English, Chairman, Associated Newspapers.

Travel: Elizabeth of Sovereign Travel in Wimbledon Village. The Wolsey Lodges.
Special Mention: Beyond the call of duty, Gerard Guerrini for all his patience and support – Mike Norriss for all his strength and knowledge – Tom Pugh for being himself – Malcolm and Rosanna Shennan for their help and kindness. Aschenputel.
The Duchess of Devonshire, The Earl of Bradford, Lady Guernsey, Major General Field, Peter Thomas and Ian Spratling.
The dust jacket: Alan Marshall of Valhaven with David Caple and Roland Martin.
ISBN Number: 0–9525410–3–3
Published: by the Beautiful Publishing Division of Good Connections Limited, Wickham House, 464 Lincoln Road, Enfield, Middlesex EN3 4AH.
E&OE should there be any incorrect accreditation please contact the above.

THE SPONSORS

British Airways.
Cartiere Burgo.
Halliburton/Brown & Root.
Kingfisher plc.
Kodak.
Merrill Lynch.
Rolls Royce plc.
Royal & SunAlliance plc.
SmithKline Beecham plc.
The Worshipful Company of Skinners.
Mamiya (Johnson's Photopia).
Sea Containers.
Simmons & Simmons.
Neil Bruce Copp.
Arsenal Football Club.
Atlantic Property Development plc.
British Tourist Authority
Canary Wharf plc.
Colt Communications plc.
DERAtec.
Dragon Systems Inc.
Harsco Corporation.
Hilton.
Historic Scotland.
ICL.
Pommery Champagne.
The Wales Tourist Board.
Wentworth.
Welsh Development Agency.
Wiltons.
Woolwich Building Society.
Xerox Corporation.
ABS (Scotland) Limited.
Adobe Systems.
British Steel.
Forbes Magazine.
British Borneo Oil & Gas plc.
High-Point Rendel.
London Export Group.
Noon Products plc.
Pacific Investments Ltd.
Simagen Ltd.
The Vintry.
Wyncote Group.
Tim & Renée Bettany.
Peter Chalk.
Dr. John Gayner.
Tim Kemp.
John A.N. Prenn
Robert & Faanya Rose.
Terrence Ruane.
Harry Ryken.
Robert Sangster.

The Horn Dance at Abbot's Bromley. Held on the Monday after September 4th. The horns have been carbon-dated – some are prehistoric. *(Staffordshire)*